MW00527657

Crystal Magic
Journal

Spells, Rituals, and Writing Prompts to
HARNESS THE POWER
OF CRYSTALS

SAMARA LAKE

WELLFLEET
PRESS

Contents

Your Crystal Journey

C rystals, a gift polished and plucked from the Earth, can be used in any way the collector desires. The beauty of crystals is that they can be worn, held, or put on a shelf, and its energies will still be felt by those who wish to connect with them.

This journal will guide you as you tap into the energies of the Moon, chakras, birthstones, and more, all within the sphere of crystal magic. To fully take advantage of the spiritual journey this practice will send you on, you must open your own energies and be willing to connect with those of the Universe. Rituals are more than just sitting and holding a crystal in your hand. Find a space where energy can flow, where your intentions can be transferred from your mind, through your hand, and onto paper to allow the crystals to release your energy into the world with a bit more precision.

Each ritual in this book either has a journal component or a prompt to help you detangle your personal energies for a clearer, more complete connection with crystals. Use the space to jot down notes and record your practice and crystal observations as you manifest your brightest desires.

As with all natural things, crystals vibrate with their unique energy and amplify the energies surrounding them. These rituals should be done while trusting your inner wisdom, but never perform them with intentions of harm or misfortune. When the messages received are muddy, trust in the Universe to bring you what you need when the time is right. Build your crystal jewel box and create a purposeful life. The energies of the world are ready to take you on your journey with crystal magic.

·FOCUS YOUR MIND·

Familiarize yourself with journaling by using these starter prompts to ready your mind for crystal magic practice.

How did you come across the magic of crystals?

What's your favorite thing about crystals?

_____

_____

_____

_____

_____

_____

_____

_____

_____

_____

_____

_____

_____

_____

A FRESH START

Evoke the beauty of labradorite and the power it brings for new beginnings and limitless potential. Say quietly or aloud:

I welcome transformation and the opportunities it brings.

What opportunities do you hope learning crystal magic will present to you?

_____

_____

_____

_____

_____

_____

_____

Intentions
& Energies

When you invite crystals into your life, journaling allows you to do so with an open, receptive heart and mind. Working with crystals is an active process of getting to know them and then tending to them to keep their energies flowing. Setting clear intentions is the first step to activating your magical powers. You can do that here with the freedom to scribble the words down as they come to you and watch them form into clear, concise intentions to manifest.

The energies of the Universe flow fluidly through pathways unseen. The pathways in you then reach out to the powers around. Crystal energies are powerful on their own, but when used with your own powerful energies, the combination is magical. Everything influences everything, but the communication is only successful when the right connections are made. With this practice, you will learn how to control those energies and detect pathways that are blocked or have gone ignored. It will take time and patience, so every time you pick up a crystal, record the process and use it as a reference.

Once you've mastered the art of setting intentions and learned the wondrous energies that make up this sparkling world, you'll be able to feel the vibrations and trust in them. Lean into your intuition and begin your spiritual journey.

◆— SETTING INTENTIONS —◆

To clearly define your intentions, answer these questions:

What do you seek?

_____

_____

_____

_____

_____

What gives you joy?

_____

_____

_____

_____

Identify where it hurts, so that you can begin to heal.

_____

_____

_____

_____

_____

_____

What might you need to let go of?

_____

_____

_____

_____

_____

_____

_____

GIVE ME GRACE

Evoke the power of amazonite to instill hope and teach you to go with the flow. Say quietly or aloud:

*I move in harmony with the Universe as I seek
to manifest a life of grace and joy.*

Where does serenity find you? Can you hear yourself in this place?

List the areas in your life where you wish to set clear intentions.
What results do you seek in these areas?

Born of the Earth, crystals surround you. Reflect on the times you
wished their energies could've guided you, but you didn't yet know
they could.

COLOR ENERGIES

Colors can help double down on your intentions, for they each have their own energies that can amplify crystal rituals. To get an extra boost from one stone, think about crystals with multiple colors, like bloodstone or labradorite.

So Many Colors!

Along with the crystals' colors, add colored candles, wear colored clothing (or makeup), drape your altar in color, or use the colors in nature to connect as many energies as you can for positive outcomes.

GET OUT OF A FUNK

Evoke the power of peridot when you feel out of step and need to re-sync to the natural rhythms of life. Say quietly or aloud:

Strength and abundance radiate from me with ease.

Reconnect with the natural world—take a walk, do a bit of gardening, or sprawl out in a patch of grass. Journal how it feels to breathe fresh air and be a part of the Earth.

_____

_____

_____

_____

_____

_____

◆—· COOL SERENITY ·—◆

Seek blue for healing, lavender for protection, bronze/brown for tranquility and stability, and black for grounding.

Write about a time when you felt your emotions were unbalanced. In what ways could you incorporate these color energies to help you?

Describe a big change you are currently experiencing in your life.
Which color would you reach for to keep you safe while navigating
this tumultuous time?

_____

_____

_____

_____

_____

_____

_____

Not The Right Color?

*If you can't find an object in the right color, substitute with a
clear-colored crystal and invoke the energies you seek.*

DARING SUNSETS

Seek red for ambition and courage, orange for communication, yellow for happiness, and pink for compassion.

When happiness and joy are in abundance, keep its companion color close. What other ways can you use these colors to create a great day?

_____

_____

_____

_____

_____

_____

_____

_____

_____

_____

_____

_____

Did you combine color energies for a greater effect? What were these combinations?

What other combinations would you use next time?

A GLOWING FUTURE

Seek gold for creativity, green for success, violet for wisdom, and purple for fertility.

Creative energy ebbs and flows, for it cannot always remain consistent. When your creativity peaks, how does it show itself to you?

_____

_____

_____

_____

_____

_____

_____

_____

_____

_____

While working on a particularly exhausting project, select a color energy to help your work progress. What helps you create?

When working toward a life-changing goal, keep a fortuitous color near your bed. Write down intentions and affirmations to keep your spirits high during this time.

CRYSTALLINE CLARITY

Seek turquoise for cleansing, gray/silver for enlightenment and dreams, and white for truth.

When your mind feels full, pick one of these colors to help cleanse it. Journal your turbulent thoughts.

When suffering nightmares, focus your mind's eye on one of the colors mentioned on the previous page to cleanse the negative energy from your head. What do you think the Universe is trying to tell you?

Some have the skill of lucid dreaming, where you can control your dreams. If you could do this, what dreams would you give yourself?

Collect
& Cleanse

*R*eady to grow your crystal collection? In your practice so far, you've learned how to set clear and concise intentions, as well as identify some of the energies in everyday life. It's finally time to turn thoughts into actions and go out into the world where crystals await you.

There are many vendors out there today, so when making your purchases, be sure to keep your energy pathways open. Go with your intuition—what calls out to you, what piques your interest, what store has collections you gravitate toward? Let the power of crystals be your guiding hand, but don't limit yourself to conventional shopping. Remember, crystals grow from the Earth. Look around you and discover what's freely available.

As you bring crystals into your sanctuary, set up your crystal altar (or altars), and learn how to cleanse them. These prompts and activities will guide you in the care of your collection, new and old.

Your crystal magic is growing. The journey ahead is full of opportunity, possibility, and beauty.

EMBRACE IT!

Evoke the warming vibrations of sunstone to open up your passion and power and allow opportunities to be revealed. Say quietly or aloud:

I radiate joy.

Write a few affirmations to uplift you whenever you feel insecure.

_____

_____

_____

_____

_____

_____

COLLECTING CRYSTALS

Start with that special crystal that speaks strongly to you, whether by an instinctive pull or the crystal's beauty, its energies, or historical use. Always remember that crystals are Mother Earth's gift to us. When buying, make sure ethical, sustainable, and fair practice has occurred. Safe harvesting should be good for the planet and its people equally.

What grounding pieces will you keep while practicing crystal magic? You can include tangible objects, words or phrases, or scents or sounds.

_____

_____

_____

_____

_____

_____

_____

_____

_____

Is there a store (either online or physical) where the energy feels right for fostering crystal magic? Describe this space's energy.

_____

_____

_____

_____

_____

Have you already spotted crystals in nature? Go to or research where they might naturally form. What does it mean to you to bring nature into your crystal sanctuary?

_____

_____

_____

_____

_____

_____

_____

CRYSTAL ALTARS

Your sanctuary needs some decoration! A crystal altar provides a visual reminder and a physical presence to help focus your energy while meditating or trying a new spell. Wherever is available to you will work—a windowsill, a cardboard box, a shelf, or a table. If you have one or multiple altars, the key is that it represents you—your heart, hopes, dreams, intentions, and life.

Here are some tricks to get your altar ready for good vibes:

- Wipe it clean with rose water.
- Sweep it with a bundle of lavender blooms.
- Use either a sage-infused cleansing spray or smoke cleanse to whisk away any energy that does not serve you.

Materials to get you started:

- Cloth—with a specific pattern, color, or texture.
- An element of nature.
- Candles or essential oils.
- Pictures of loved ones.

MAKE IT SPARKLE

Evoke the cleansing power of a sapphire-infused elixir to purify your altar or other sacred spaces.

Instructions:

1. Place the sapphire—or clear quartz if you don't have sapphire—in a bowl of shallow water.

2. Place the bowl on your altar where natural light will touch it.

3. Sprinkle a salt ring around the bowl.

4. Light a candle, preferably one in the cleansing color of blue.

Say quietly or aloud:

I will reach for the heavens until I touch the stars.

Do you like to organize or clean? What are the positives to mundane tasks such as these?

_____

_____

_____

_____

_____

Have you dabbled in other magical practices before now? How will you include them in your crystal practice or on your altar(s)?

_____

_____

_____

_____

_____

Are you a minimalist? Do you like color? Do you favor wacky trinkets? Brainstorm styles or objects you could include on your altar.

_____

_____

_____

_____

_____

CRYSTAL CLEANSES

To properly invite new crystals into your sanctuary and personal practice, you must first cleanse them; after the first time, cleansing occurs only when needed. The role of a cleanse is to prepare the crystal for rituals and intentions. Once your intentions change, or have manifested, another cleanse should be performed.

Do you make New Year's resolutions? Much like setting intentions, if you have set resolutions, write them down here.

_____

_____

_____

_____

_____

_____

_____

NEED A MOMENT?

Evoke the revitalizing power of garnet to balance your energy and restore your courage. Say quietly or aloud:

I step bravely into discomfort, for that is where I grow.

A reset day is when you wash off the past days, months, or years to start anew mentally and physically. When would a reset day help you? What would you do?

_____

_____

_____

_____

_____

_____

· MOONLIGHT CLEANSE ·

The Moon's energetic glow can cleanse all crystals. Place your crystal where it'll receive the Moon's light and leave it overnight.

Plan a night to stargaze, whether outside, or inside, looking out your window. Afterwards, journal how stargazing with no distractions improved your connection to the Universe.

⟵ WATER CLEANSE ⟶

If a crystal is water resistant, dip it in a cool water bath to cleanse, or do a mindful rinse under running water while visualizing negativity washing away.

Dip your hands in the water; feel the temperature. Mindfully, think about how water affects you, focusing on its texture and sound.

....

....

....

....

....

WATER RESISTANT?

Crystals rated 7 or higher on the Mohs hardness scale are usually safe.

◆── SALT CLEANSE ──◆

Create a bed of salt (table salt, kosher salt, sea salt) about 2 inches thick in a container. Lay your crystals in the salt and let them cleanse for at least 30 minutes, or overnight.

What negativity will this salt cleanse get rid of? Think about the energies in the crystal you are cleansing, as well as the energies in yourself.

RULE OF SALT

Porous crystals, crystals that contain iron, or those that contain water are NOT good candidates for this method. If you're unsure about your crystals' suitability, place the crystals you wish to cleanse into a glass bowl, and set that bowl into the salt.

EARTH CLEANSE

Ensure the spot is safe, then mark the location. Bury the crystals in the ground or in a flowerpot filled with clean soil. For the best results, leave overnight under a Full Moon.

Write your gratitude to Mother Earth in the form of a letter.

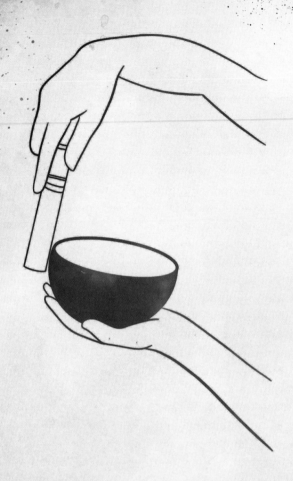

·VIBRATIONAL CLEANSE·

Get creative and have fun with this one. Rituals can include the sound of your voice in a chant or song passing over the crystals. Strike a gong, ring a chime, play a crystal or brass singing bowl, or play your favorite music. Use vibrational sounds that are pleasing to you.

What are some of your favorite songs or sounds? Does sound play a role in your practice?

Scrying & Moon Magic

As you go on your crystal magic journey, it is natural to want to peek into the future. With crystals being one of the many energies of the world, their powers have a wide span. Crystal scrying, also called crystal gazing, is an act of divination by staring into a reflective surface for images or visions. Feel free to get a little creative in this part of the journal, and draw images in the blank spaces of what the Universe shows you.

Because nighttime is the suggested time to scry, this section will also include an element of Moon magic. Specifically, it will show you how you can align your intentions to the phases of the Moon and the energies it exudes throughout any given month.

For this section, grab a pencil, a scrying bowl, and a calendar of the upcoming moon phases. Through the guidance of crystals, get ready to enhance your nighttime routine.

SAY IT LIKE YOU MEAN IT!

Evoke the power of the majestic clear quartz for an energy boost.
Say quietly or aloud:

It is clear: I am beautiful. I am wise. I am love. I am light. I am enough.

Finish these mantras for self-love.

I am _____

_____

I can _____

_____

I love _____

_____

_____

A quiet space is most ideal for scrying. Draw or describe your quiet place. What is its significance?

CRYSTAL SCRYING

Scrying allows you to delve into the past, see the present more clearly, or predict what the future holds. Many tools can be used for this form of divination, such as the oft-gazed crystal ball and other reflective objects like mirrors, candle flames, and water. Clear crystals or dark polished stones are the best conduits for scrying.

To prepare, follow these steps:

1. Place the crystal somewhere you can sit comfortably.

2. Center yourself by acknowledging the problem or intention.

3. Softly gaze into your crystal.

4. Keep a clear mind and a gentle focus.

*What other methods of divination, if any, have you tried
in order to seek answers about the future? How do you feel
regarding divination?*

_____

_____

_____

_____

_____

*What are some events from your past that you wish to learn from,
understand, or see from a different point of view?*

_____

_____

_____

_____

_____

Regarding your future, what are you most curious about?

After scrying, take the time to write down or draw the messages you received and any thoughts that occurred to you.

THE PHASES OF THE MOON

Moon magic is its own magical practice, but from a crystal magic perspective, the Moon is just one large crystal in the sky. Its changing phases produce energies that wax and wane over the course of a month-long cycle. Attune to those energies, and incorporate crystals to magnify, align, or even tame them for an eclipsing month of manifesting intentions.

What knowledge do you already have about the Moon? Do you keep track of its phases or the different Full Moons over the months?

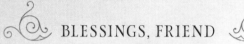

BLESSINGS, FRIEND

Evoke the healing and protective power of selenite and honor the Greek Moon goddess Selene. Say quietly or aloud:

I trust my inner wisdom and will listen to my heart, for it speaks the ancient truth of my guardian spirits.

Do you believe in guardian spirits to make sure events in your life are meaningful and aligned with the Universe's plan? If not, what do you believe?

_____

_____

_____

_____

_____

What kind of energy do you wish to imbue into the world? How do you hope the Moon will help?

_____

_____

_____

_____

_____

_____

NIGHTTIME RITUALS

Connect with the energies of the Moon's phases by performing a ritual, meditation, or spell when the Moon is high. The crystals listed in the next few prompts are companions to help you reach the Moon wherever it is in the sky.

57

→ · NEW MOON · ←

Green jade, labradorite, tiger's eye.

A New Moon brings the opportunity for new beginnings. What do you intend to start doing?

_____

_____

_____

_____

_____

_____

_____

→ · WAXING CRESCENT · →

Carnelian, garnet, rose quartz.

It is time to refine intentions and consider the actions needed to manifest them. What intentions are you changing, and how will you begin working toward them?

← · FIRST QUARTER · →

Aquamarine, red jasper, sunstone.

Realize intentions as energies build during the first quarter. In this highly inspirational period, journal your current thoughts and ideas before it gets too chaotic in your mind.

·— · WAXING GIBBOUS · —·

Citrine, tiger's eye, turquoise.

In this waiting period, don't lose faith. Describe a time you almost lost faith but didn't and saw your perseverance pay off.

← · FULL MOON · →

Green aventurine, moonstone, selenite.

The Full Moon is a time for celebration. How do you feel about the goals you've recently achieved? How will you celebrate?

→ · WANING GIBBOUS · →

Amethyst, black tourmaline, sapphire.

What lessons and discoveries have you made from a deeper connection with the Moon?

→ · LAST QUARTER · →

Blue lace agate, malachite, obsidian.

It's time for self-care and a recharge. A lot has changed, so go and treat yourself for your triumphs. Divulge your guilty pleasures or ideal "cheat" day.

WANING CRESCENT

Bloodstone, pink tourmaline, rose quartz.

Remember, it's a cycle. Take some time to jot down your gratitude for the many cycles of life.

_____

_____

_____

_____

_____

_____

_____

_____

Meditations
& Chakras

The abundance of energies that flow through the Universe can be quite chaotic at times, especially when first learning how to navigate their winding pathways. Humans, both in tune to their magic and not, forget to stop and slow down, often getting distracted by a cluttered mind and reacting without purpose. When it comes to listening to energies and communing with the Universe, a practitioner must focus the mind and let their deepest desires speak for themselves. The best results are often found through patience and trust.

Open up to the voices of the world and hear the ones you wish to connect with through meditation. This is a calming practice to help you invite positive energies into your crystal sanctuary and receive the answers you have awaited. There are loud and soft voices alike, and they require the space and time to speak with you in confidence. Quiet your mind, hold tight to your intentions, and reach for the crystals that will amplify what you seek.

Meditation will also ready you to open your chakras and the life force they provide for your mind, body, and spirit. Chakras make up a large part of the energies within you, and through meditation you will come to understand them. As you tread upon the tranquil path of meditation, and your chakras have cleared and are performing at their best, become the conductor of prime energy flow.

 # AHEM, ATTENTION, PLEASE

Evoke the energies of hematite as you start your journey through meditation. Say quietly or aloud:

I am grounded and focused and live mindfully each day.

What does it mean to live mindfully? How will your life change when you are more mindful of the Universe?

CRYSTAL MEDITATION

Meditation means to engage in a mental exercise to reach a heightened level of spiritual awareness and become mindful and present. Incorporating crystals in meditation gives you a tangible anchor and can deepen your meditative state.

In your crystal sanctuary, situate yourself in a comfortable position, and open your mind.

1. Choose the crystal whose energy you wish to use and release into your life.

2. Gently hold it in your hands; feel its shape, weight, temperature, and texture.

3. Absorb its color energy.

4. Visualize the crystal's energy flowing into you while your energy and intentions flow back into the crystal.

DON'T HAVE THE RIGHT CRYSTAL?

Clear quartz can stand in for any stone's magical essence.

Meditate with bronze's clarity of thought. What messages did you receive from within and around you?

Meditate with the awareness of turquoise. What situations do you wish to be more present in?

_____

_____

_____

_____

_____

_____

_____

Meditate with the peace from white. Describe what would bring you peace right now or in this period of your life.

_____

_____

_____

_____

_____

THE SEVEN MAJOR CHAKRAS

Chakras act as the gateway to your physical, emotional, and spiritual well-being, and when they are not taken care of it causes problems with your mind, body, and spirit. If a chakra is blocked, your magical energy is blocked, too. Practice opening and activating the seven major chakras using chakra meditation. Combine the breathing and intentional movements you have learned to tune into your chakras.

ROOT

Focuses your meditation work and spellwork.

SACRAL, OR PELVIC

Opens your connection to others.

SOLAR PLEXUS

Aids your call to action in manifesting intentions.

HEART

Helps with all manner of love spells.

THROAT

Keeps your intentions clear, your
spellwork articulate.

THIRD EYE

Manages your witchy intuition.

CROWN

Coordinates magic beyond the physical realm.

During meditation, place your hand, or crystal, at the base of your spine. Relax your body as you picture a flower blooming.

Crystal companions: black tourmaline, garnet, obsidian.

How can you take advantage of the strengths you already have to help you tackle your weaknesses?

_____

_____

_____

_____

_____

_____

_____

_____

_____

_____

_____

_____

SACRAL, OR PELVIC

During meditation, place your hand, or crystal, just below your navel. Picture a stream of your raw feelings unraveling into the world.

Crystal companions: carnelian, garnet, sunstone.

Name a person in your life, aloud or in your head. Then, close your eyes and select the crystal that calls to you. Does the crystal's energy reflect your relationship with that person, or do you seek to emulate it?

_____

_____

_____

_____

_____

_____

_____

During meditation, place your hand, or crystal, between the navel and ribcage. Feel your body warm as the fire of confidence fills you.

Crystal companions: amber, moonstone, tiger's eye.

Reflect on the person you used to be before being mindful of this energy-packed Universe. Are you content in who you are now? Why or why not?

_____

_____

_____

_____

_____

_____

_____

HEART

During meditation, place your hand, or crystal, on the center of your chest. Breathe deeply and picture the blood flowing love and forgiveness through your veins.

Crystal companions: emerald, green tourmaline, ruby.

Do you appreciate your unique heart? What are the positives to being compassionate and loving?

_____

_____

_____

_____

_____

_____

_____

_____

During meditation, hum in varying tones and measures to allow the vibrations to clear your throat chakra.

Crystal companions: aquamarine, opal, turquoise.

What piece of wisdom have you gained through crystal magic that you would like to share with others? How do you think crystal magic can help someone in your life?

_____

_____

_____

_____

_____

_____

_____

_____

THIRD EYE

During meditation, close your eyes and focus your attention to the center of your forehead. Train your mind's eye to remain open.

Crystal companions: celestite, moldavite, sapphire.

Have you ever connected with the unseen world before? What happened that enabled you to finally see it?

_____

_____

_____

_____

_____

_____

_____

_____

CROWN

During meditation, move your hands, palms up, in an arch. Push them up from your sternum, then open them wide over your head. Repeat the movement until you feel calm and receptive.

Crystal companions: amethyst, selenite, tanzanite.

What crystal allies boost the connections you've made with the Universe? What other methods have you found strengthen your connections?

CHAKRA RAINBOW MEDITATION

Chakras are our own personal links to the magical energies of the rainbow. They can help when selecting crystals and sharpening your alignment to them. It's time to draw on two exterior energy pathways at the same time. Believe that you can listen to both crystal and color energy as you look through the perspective of your chakras. Pick up a crystal of the intentional color, open your chakras, and feel the energies vitalize you.

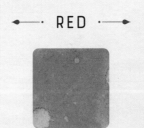

RED

Breathe in passion; breathe out pain.

What we are passionate about can also bring us pain. What was a difficult experience you really struggled through? If you knew how things would turn out, would you make the same decisions?

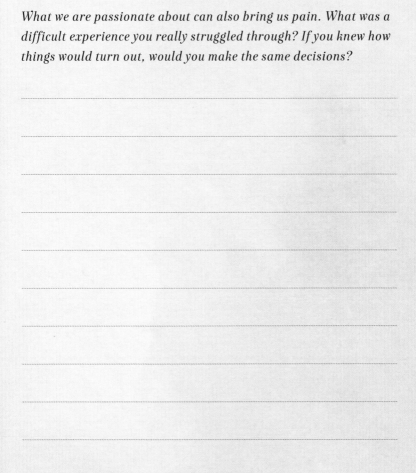

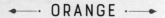

ORANGE

Breathe in creativity; breathe out boredom.

What do you want to create that you haven't allowed yourself to? What's stopping you? Then, do some research, and see how you can make it work.

·— · YELLOW · —·

Breathe in the joyful, life-giving qualities of the Sun; breathe out fear.

Put a toe out of your comfort zone—take a spontaneous trip, tackle a challenging recipe, reach out to that person you have been too scared to contact. Journal your experience.

GREEN

Breathe in renewal; breathe out sorrow.

Do a bit of reorganizing, like feng shui, and witness the space now opened to new ideas. When, or in what areas of your life, have you intentionally changed in order to grow?

_____

_____

_____

_____

_____

_____

_____

_____

BLUE

Breathe in calm; breathe out tension.

Take the time to relax your body by meditating, watching a movie, or taking a bath. What are the small things in life you do for yourself? Are you doing them often enough?

INDIGO

Breathe in intuition; breathe out negativity.

For any kind of magical practice to work, you must first believe in yourself. Write about the positives of your unique self.

_____

_____

_____

_____

_____

_____

_____

_____

_____

Breathe in the messages of the Universe; breathe out gratitude.

Find three items to represent the Earth, Sun, and Moon that you can carry with you today. What are they, and how do they keep you connected to these celestial beings?

_____

_____

_____

_____

_____

_____

_____

_____

_____

_____

_____

_____

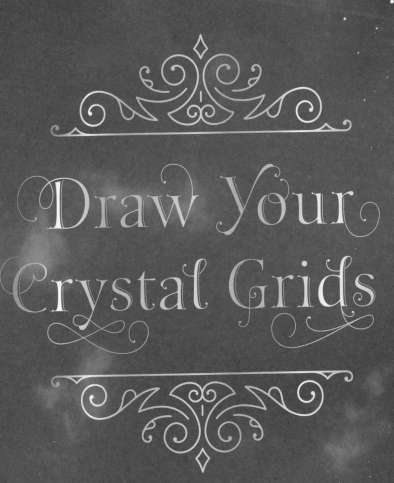

Draw Your Crystal Grids

*J*ournaling crystal magic requires more than just space to write down crystal names, intentions, and the results that the Universe sends through newly opened energy pathways. Because this magic uses tangible objects and is more than just visualizing energy, this section will include drawing space for you to get creative and illustrate your crystal rituals.

The setup of your rituals, especially when using more than one crystal, is called a crystal grid—a structured energy pathway that best allows your intentions to come to fruition or to conjure more complex energies into your life. The alignment, synergies, and amplifications of the crystal energies, your intentions, the grid's shape, and the Universe, kick crystal magic into high gear in a controlled manner.

Think about how you organize your desk, the furniture in your bedroom, or the books on your shelf. This is intuitive work you can't get wrong. Listen to the crystals, interpret their best energy pathways, and use the shapes that call out to you.

Journal the energies you wish to have in this period of your life.

Journal the energies you wish to always be present in your life.

⦚ KEEP YOUR CHIN UP ⦚

Evoke the power of black onyx to help intentions take root when so many are surfacing at once. Say quietly or aloud:

I embrace the darkness, for that is when I see the light.

There are infinite possibilities when accepting the unknown. How do you approach ambiguous situations? Are you content in the face of the unknown?

....

....

....

....

....

....

GRID SETUP AND ACTIVATION

The first step, always, is to know your intention. Take a moment to center yourself, your breathing, and check in with your heart. Listen to the Universe and feel the energies coursing through and around you. Align your intentions to your purpose, then . . .

- Choose your center point crystal—the crystal whose energies are best suited for the purpose of the ritual.
- Arrange additional crystals that will build up your purpose.
- Hold your dominant hand over the center stone and feel the energy vibrations.
- Move your hand deliberately over each crystal in the desired direction.

WHICH WAY SHOULD I GO?

To draw something to you, such as abundance, creativity, love, etc., activate your grid in a clockwise direction. To keep something away, activate the grid in a counterclockwise direction.

What thoughts, objects, or people have you found block positive energy pathways?

_____

_____

_____

_____

_____

_____

_____

_____

_____

_____

_____

_____

Write a short message to yourself reminding you to be open and accepting to the energies around you.

— DRAW YOUR CRYSTAL GRIDS —

Crystal grids are energy pathways constructed by your crystals.
When organizing a ritual, place the crystals in a shape of
significance in regard to your intentions. Start by laying out your
crystals in a symmetrical shape. This arrangement should be
purposeful and take geometric forms. Use the drawing space
on the next page to illustrate your crystal grid. You can label the
name and location of each crystal so you can recreate it next time.

Crystals used: _____

_____

_____

Intentions: _____

_____

_____

My experience: _____

_____

_____

_____

_____

_____

Try another geometric shape for this grid.

Crystals used: _____

_____

_____

Intentions: _____

_____

_____

_____

My experience: _____

_____

_____

_____

_____

_____

_____

_____

Sacred geometry formations—patterns spoken in the language of mathematics—exist everywhere in nature. Use the cross to start with. On each grid, draw or label the crystal you used in the designated spaces.

Cross

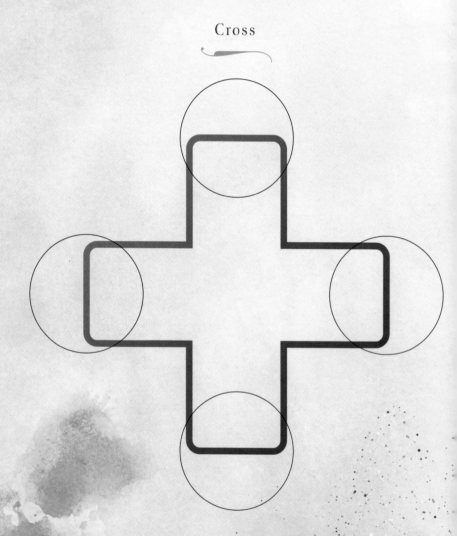

Crystals used: _____

_____

_____

_____

Intentions: _____

_____

_____

_____

My experience: _____

_____

_____

_____

_____

_____

_____

_____

_____

_____

Tetrahedron (Pyramid)

Crystals used: _____

_____

_____

_____

Intentions: _____

_____

_____

_____

My experience: _____

_____

_____

_____

_____

_____

_____

_____

_____

Do you plan your days or let them unravel on their own?

_____

_____

_____

_____

_____

Do you like following pre-written guidelines, or do you let your intuition take charge when completing a task?

_____

_____

_____

_____

_____

Take some time to write about new insights you have gained about your life from practicing crystal magic.

CREATE YOUR OWN GRIDS

Crystal grids change often, depending on intentions, desires, and the crystals themselves. Spend the next pages sketching grids you want to use, have used, or would like to use again, either in a specific shape or freestyled.

Grid title: ....

Crystals used: ....

....

....

Intentions: ....

....

....

My experience: ....

....

....

....

....

....

....

Grid title: _____

Crystals used: _____

_____

_____

Intentions: _____

_____

_____

_____

_____

My experience: _____

_____

_____

_____

_____

_____

_____

_____

_____

Crystals & Birthstones

While working with crystals, we cannot forget the significance of the twelve gemstones that sit on a throne throughout an entire month of exceptional power. These specific gemstones, or birthstones, are the sisters in the crystal family. They possess formidable energies in correspondence to a predestined power month. Learning how to use them properly will only enhance your crystal practice.

If you haven't already, incorporate your individual birthstone into your crystal magic to increase good vibrational energies. All year long, add the gem to your altar(s), and keep the gem near during rituals or where its energies can constantly be felt, but don't forget about the remaining birthstones. As a general rule, birthstones can be incorporated in spells and rituals during their power months, or when a gemstone's energy best suits your intention. It's similar to using crystals, except the birthstones' power may be limited if used outside of their time frame, so be sure to plan accordingly.

Keep track of the information you learn during the months when using their birthstones. If you trial combinations—pair crystals and birthstones or your birthstone with another—record the results. Just like the phases of the Moon, aligning energies together when they are at their peak will produce more complex results. Moving forward in this journal, become in tune with the patterns of the Universe.

WHAT A GEM

Evoke the high vibrations of moldavite to help raise not only your energy but also the energy of other stones around it. Say quietly or aloud:

I emerge from the fire, reborn of the stars. I accept healing energy into my life.

Have you researched birthstones? If so, what is your relationship with your birthstone? If not, what do you hope to learn?

· JANUARY—GARNET ·

Believed to keep its wearer safe while traveling, garnet has a powerfully energizing and revitalizing energy; it also purifies and invites love and devotion.

January's magical practice: _____

_____

_____

On my altar(s): _____

_____

Combinations with garnet: _____

_____

Other notes: _____

_____

_____

_____

Amethyst builds relationships, has a strong healing and calming vibration, boosts inner strength, and offers spiritual protection.

February's magical practice: _____

_____

_____

On my altar(s): _____

_____

Combinations with amethyst: _____

_____

Other notes: _____

_____

_____

_____

MARCH—AQUAMARINE

Aquamarine's energies help release anger, relieve stress, and raise the tides of courage to withstand whatever life throws at you.

March's magical practice: _____
_____
_____

On my altar(s): _____
_____

Combinations with aquamarine: _____
_____

Other notes: _____
_____
_____
_____

·APRIL—DIAMOND·

The diamond is believed to instill courage as well as standing as a symbol of everlasting love. However, a diamond worn for effect or prestige will bring the opposite of love.

April's magical practice: _____

_____

_____

On my altar(s): _____

_____

Combinations with diamond: _____

_____

Other notes: _____

_____

_____

_____

← · MAY—EMERALD · →

A sign of wisdom, growth, and patience, the emerald helps release negative energy and opens your heart to love and the power of inner strength.

May's magical practice: ....

....

....

On my altar(s): ....

....

Combinations with emerald: ....

....

Other notes: ....

....

....

....

JUNE—PEARL

The pearl is a traditional symbol of purity and inner wisdom. While not a true crystal, pearls can be worn to magnify loyalty, truth, and sincerity.

June's magical practice: _____

_____

_____

On my altar(s): _____

_____

Combinations with pearl: _____

_____

Other notes: _____

_____

_____

_____

JULY—RUBY

Ruby's glorious red color symbolizes love and passion and promotes energy, sensuality, and vitality.

July's magical practice: ....

....

....

On my altar(s): ....

....

Combinations with ruby: ....

....

Other notes: ....

....

....

....

AUGUST—PERIDOT

A symbol of strength, peridot ushers in prosperity and peace.

August's magical practice: ....

....

....

On my altar(s): ....

....

Combinations with peridot: ....

....

Other notes: ....

....

....

....

← · SEPTEMBER—SAPPHIRE · →

Another symbol of purity and wisdom, sapphire has a calming energy. Work with it to strengthen belief in yourself and foster self-esteem.

September's magical practice: _____

_____

_____

On my altar(s): _____

_____

Combinations with sapphire: _____

_____

Other notes: _____

_____

_____

_____

← · OCTOBER–OPAL · →

The opal represents faithfulness and confidence. This stone encourages creativity and emits a protective aura.

October's magical practice: _____

_____

_____

On my altar(s): _____

_____

Combinations with opal: _____

_____

Other notes: _____

_____

_____

_____

NOVEMBER—TOPAZ

Symbolizing love and affection, topaz promotes honesty and openness.

November's magical practice: _____

_____

_____

On my altar(s): _____

_____

Combinations with topaz: _____

_____

Other notes: _____

_____

_____

_____

·⎯⎯· DECEMBER—TURQUOISE ·⎯⎯·

Turquoise brings luck and good fortune. This healing stone heightens your spiritual attunement and promotes clear communication and forgiveness.

December's magical practice: _____

_____

_____

On my altar(s): _____

_____

Combinations with turquoise: _____

_____

Other notes: _____

_____

_____

_____

Your Crystal Rituals

hroughout this journal, the prompts and activities have allowed you to test prestructured rituals as well as create some of your own. Setting intentions guides you to better interpret your inner wisdom and know all that you desire to manifest. Even if you haven't noticed, your confidence in crystal magic has grown. You know how to navigate energy pathways and listen to the Universe. The tools you've collected have enhanced your skill set and made you flexible in your practice. After everything you've experienced, be proud of how far you've come.

You may still be at the beginning of your journey, but even if you aren't, the following rituals should be added to your treasury for safekeeping. For those specific, recurring intentions, they will be essential rituals you use over and over again. Intentions are personal to you, so they will be focused on your mood, self-empowerment, and personal guidance as you continue to transcend.

Follow your intuition and thrive in the connections you've made with the Universe so far. Remember to always use crystal magic with positive and kind intentions, and record the magic happening at your fingertips.

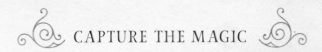

CAPTURE THE MAGIC

Evoke the healing power of peacock ore to help channel your inner energies. Say quietly or aloud:

I choose to see beyond that which is physical; I believe in the power of magic.

Spend some time defining your inner energies. What do they look like, feel like, sound like, etc.?

Describe your current daily, seasonal, or yearly routine.

_____

_____

_____

_____

_____

_____

_____

Do you like to change your routines or stick to one proven path?

_____

_____

_____

_____

_____

_____

_____

Do you practice crystal magic outside of your sanctuary? This might be at your place of work, while traveling, or in nature. Reflect on why you do or do not.

⌇ **CRYSTAL MAGIC ON THE GO** ⌇

Crystal magic should be practiced when it best fits your schedule,
but the times we need it most are often when we have no time.
Meditative crystal rituals do not have to be time-consuming or
elaborate. They are intended to work for and with you. When time
is of the essence, gather your thoughts, some crystals, and thirty
seconds to do some quick magic.

STRESS RELIEF

To center yourself during a stressful time, jot down what you wish to gain from the situation you're about to walk into.

In your mode of transportation, think about your destination. How will you remain connected to the Universe when you arrive? Jot down some methods beforehand.

MOODS

There is no quick fix to controlling self-righteous moods, but crystal energies can help you detect and better understand them. Think of them as mentors teaching you how to achieve your desired state of mind. Follow these next rituals when you need help navigating your mood swings.

HOW TO USE RITUALS

With each ritual, the crystals mentioned hold the energies you seek. Use them in your grids, place them on your altar(s), or do a simple spell with them. These rituals are meant to be pulled out of the vault whenever needed.

SLEEP

Amethyst, celestite, and selenite provide calming, balancing, and soothing vibrations and can help purify any negative energy around or within you.

Do you sleep with white noise or nature sounds in the background? What are some necessities for a good night's sleep?

PATIENCE

Amber, emerald, and sapphire are excellent crystal companions for fostering patience.

Utilize meditation techniques you previously learned. To help you find patience, come up with a 3-5-step process that includes breathing, counting, and a crystal.

CONFIDENCE

For those times when a little "fake it till you make it" is required, choose agate, carnelian, or opal.

In what areas of life do you think your confidence lacks the most? Why do you think it happens here?

FORGIVENESS

Whether it's yourself you're striving to forgive or someone close to you, or you're seeking that all-healing forgiveness from another, rhodochrosite can help.

What mistake made by someone else do you recognize and are now willing to forgive? If you cannot forgive now, what are some other ways to find closure?

← · RELEASE · →

Amethyst has your back when you just can't shake those worries loose.

Create a spell that uses amethyst to help ease your worries.
Use the following to help you get started:

ᖕ What is your intention?

ᖕ What kind of physical manifestation will result?

ᖕ Is there a symbolic representation?

_____

_____

_____

_____

_____

_____

_____

_____

_____

_____

_____

CREATIVITY

The ancient, double-terminated Herkimer diamond is able to transmit as well as receive information beyond any that we know, helping you open up to new ideas through divine inspiration.

What's the last craft activity you tried? How did it expand your creativity?

_____

_____

_____

_____

_____

_____

_____

_____

_____

_____

_____

EMPOWERMENT

Crystals are beautiful companions that boost your confidence like a pair of well-fitted jeans. They empower you with their beauty, but it's their energies that can bring you into spiritual alignment and show you just how powerful you truly are. Find that extra boost in these next rituals.

What makes you feel empowered, whether it's an activity, a skill you've mastered, or a personal trait?

_____

_____

_____

_____

_____

_____

_____

_____

_____

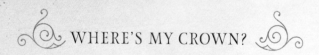

WHERE'S MY CROWN?

Evoke the power of carnelian to increase your personal power and confidence. Say quietly or aloud:

I act with the passion of purpose.

Do you wish to take on more leadership roles? Does being in charge empower you?

_____

_____

_____

_____

_____

_____

→ · TRUTH AND TRUST · →

When you need an ally to hold you accountable for your truth or give you the courage to trust your truth as well as those told to you, turn to your favorite blue crystals.

In the security of a ritual circle, spill your truths, love them, and trust the Universe to use them to your benefit. Write what this freedom means to you.

Invite tiger's eye to boost your strength when the stakes are high and your nerves are getting in the way.

What makes you competitive? What's the difference between healthy and unhealthy competition?

SUCCESS

Pyrite manifests tangible results that are proof of your success.

Write down a goal you wish to manifest. What are your action steps?

_____

_____

_____

_____

_____

Track your progress here.

_____

_____

_____

_____

_____

EMBRACE YOUR INNER GODDESS

Use crystal magic to connect to your goddess aura with these combinations:

REALM OF POWER	GODDESS	CRYSTAL
Love & Beauty	Aphrodite (Greek)	Rose quartz
Marriage, Fertility & Motherhood	Isis (Egyptian)	Carnelian
Relationships, Truth & Forgiveness	Rhiannon (Welsh)	Sapphire
Home, Hearth & Healing	Bao Gu (Chinese)	Clear quartz
Abundance, Good Fortune & Prosperity	Lakshmi (Hindu)	Diamond
Wisdom & Knowledge	Snotra (Norse)	A small pile of rocks or stones

Define your goddess aura. Choose from the table on the previous page or do your own research. What do you envision when you think about practicing with the power of a divine being?

⌒ GUIDANCE ⌒

Whether holding your hand while walking beside you, or taking the lead as you follow their paths, crystal energies can be your greatest guides when it comes to understanding a situation and how the Universe is working. Think of your crystal as the device that calls upon your very own fairy godmother when you're in need of a guiding hand.

From whom in your life do you seek guidance and why?

_____

_____

_____

_____

_____

_____

_____

_____

_____

_____

LISTEN CLOSELY

Evoke the power of celestite to seek divine guidance and enhance your mindfulness. Say quietly or aloud:

If I can dream it, I can live it.

It's okay to not want help in a situation, but sometimes we need it. When have you refused help you should've accepted? How did this experience go?

_____

_____

_____

_____

_____

_____

— · INTUITION · —

Call on the energy of lapis lazuli to make your intuition heard.

When you feel doubtful, put your walls down and let your intuition pour out. When do you doubt yourself?

_____

_____

_____

_____

_____

What makes you doubt yourself?

_____

_____

_____

_____

_____

_____

← · TRAVEL TALISMANS · →

Choose a crystal to take with you on your next journey.

- AMETHYST to combat stressful emotions.
- GARNET for safe travel.
- GREEN JADE for good luck.
- MOONSTONE for adapting to the ebb and flow of changing schedules and routines.
- SPIRIT QUARTZ to open your mind and heart to new experiences.

Where do you want to travel next? How do you feel about traveling in general?

_____

_____

_____

_____

_____

_____

_____

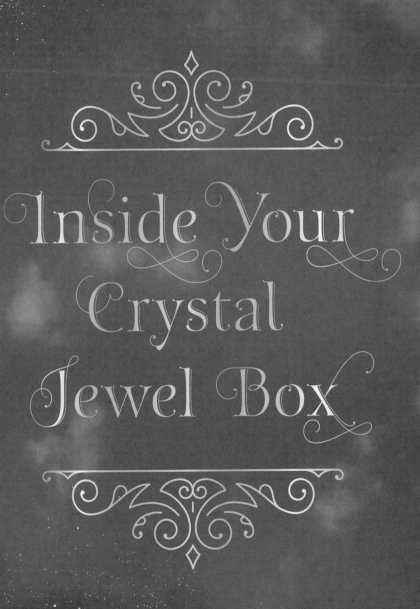

Inside Your Crystal Jewel Box

I hope that this journal has been able to help you manifest your desired level of spirituality, as well as enhance your magical practice. As this practice may be ever-growing, I would like to leave you some inventory space to catalog the most prized possessions of your collection. Beside each entry, place a picture of your crystal, or draw it to the best of your abilities. Add details such as the date it was collected and where you stumbled upon it. In the notes, record the ways you like to practice with it, describing the journey you and the crystal have been on already, or what kind of future you have planned with it now in your life.

Continue collecting and learning. Above all, never forget the sense of peace and fulfillment you get when you align desires, thoughts, and actions through the beauty of crystal magic.

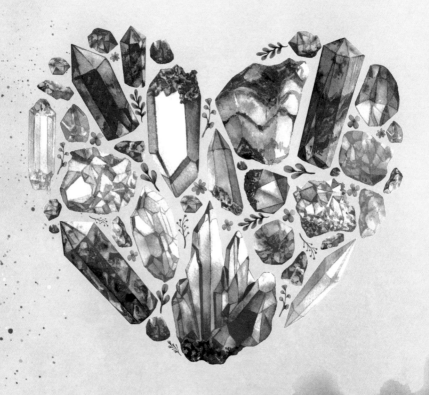

Crystal:

Date Collected:

Color:

Origin:

Notes:

Crystal:

Date Collected:

Color:

Origin:

Notes:

Crystal: _____

Date Collected: _____

Color: _____

Origin: _____

Notes: _____

_____

_____

_____

Crystal: _____

Date Collected: _____

Color: _____

Origin: _____

Notes: _____

_____

_____

_____

Crystal:_____

Date Collected:_____

Color:_____

Origin:_____

Notes:_____

_____

_____

_____

_____

Crystal:_____

Date Collected:_____

Color:_____

Origin:_____

Notes:_____

_____

_____

_____

© 2023 Quarto Publishing Group USA Inc.

First published in 2023 by Wellfleet Press, an imprint of The Quarto Group, 142 West 36th Street, 4th Floor, New York, NY 10018, USA
T (212) 779-4972 F (212) 779-6058
www.Quarto.com

Contains content previously published in 2022 as *Crystal Magic* by Wellfleet Press, an imprint of The Quarto Group, 142 West 36th Street, 4th Floor, New York, NY 10018, USA.

Wellfleet titles are also available at discount for retail, wholesale, promotional, and bulk purchase. For details, contact the Special Sales Manager by email at specialsales@quarto.com or by mail at The Quarto Group, Attn: Special Sales Manager, 100 Cummings Center Suite 265D, Beverly, MA 01915 USA

10 9 8 7 6 5 4 3 2 1

ISBN: 978-1-57715-337-5

Publisher: Rage Kindelsperger
Creative Director: Laura Drew
Senior Managing Editor: Cara Donaldson
Editorial Assistant: Katelynn Abraham
Additional Text: Mary J. Cassells
Cover and Interior Design: Sydney Martenis

Printed in China